MUSIC FROM
A CHARLIE BROWN CHRISTMAS

MUSIC BY VINCE GUARALDI, WORDS BY LEE MENDELSON
ARRANGED FOR HARP BY SYLVIA WOODS

A Charlie Brown Christmas was the first prime-time animated TV special based upon Charles Schulz's beloved *Peanuts* characters. Since its CBS debut in 1965, it has aired in the USA every Christmas season.

Christmas Time Is Here - page 1 and 3

In the TV special, A Charlie Brown Christmas, *Christmas Time Is Here* was sung by members of the choir of St. Paul's Episcopal Church in San Rafael, California.

If you play pedal harp, or if your lever harp is tuned to the key of C or 1 or 2 flats, play the version on page 1. If your lever harp is tuned to 3 flats, play the arrangement on page 3.

Both of these arrangements require quite a few sharping lever changes within the music.

Linus and Lucy - page 5 and 7

Linus and Lucy was originally released on the Vince Guaraldi Trio's album "Jazz Impressions of a Boy Named Charlie Brown" in 1964. It was used in the TV special A Charlie Brown Christmas, and has been featured in many subsequent specials. This happy dance tune is the most-recognized theme song of the *Peanuts* characters.

There are 2 arrangements of *Linus and Lucy*. Once you set your sharping levers at the beginning, there are no lever changes needed in either version.

The intermediate arrangement on page 5 includes 2-note chords in the right hand. The easier arrangement on page 7 has the main melody as single notes.

The left hand is basically the same in both arrangements, except that the easier version is written an octave higher so it can be played on smaller harps.

Christmas Time Is Here

FROM A CHARLIE BROWN CHRISTMAS

for pedal harps and lever harps tuned to C

Music by VINCE GUARALDI
Words by LEE MENDELSON
Harp arrangement by SYLVIA WOODS

This arrangement is for pedal harps and for lever harps tuned to the key of C or 1 or 2 flats.
    If your lever harp is tuned to 3 flats, play the arrangement on page 3.

Lever harp players: set your sharping levers for the key signature, and then re-set the levers shown above.
Sharping lever changes are indicated with diamond notes and also with octave wording.
The lever changes marked with an * in measures 10, 21 and 27 need to be flipped just a split second before the note is played.

Pedal changes are written below the bass staff.

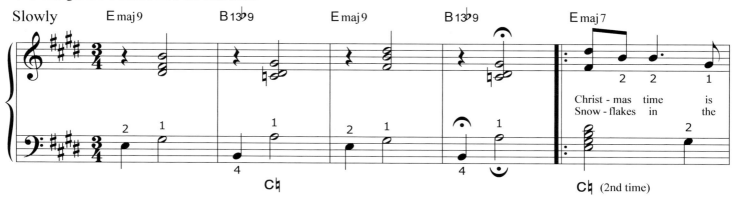

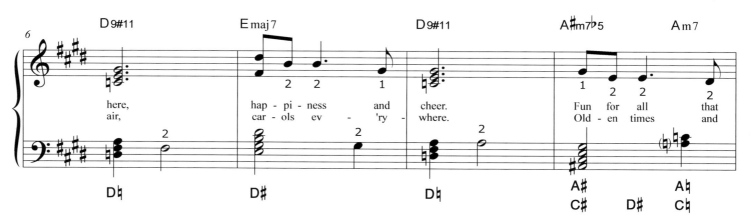

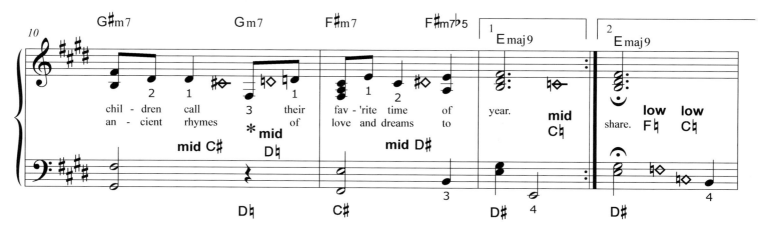

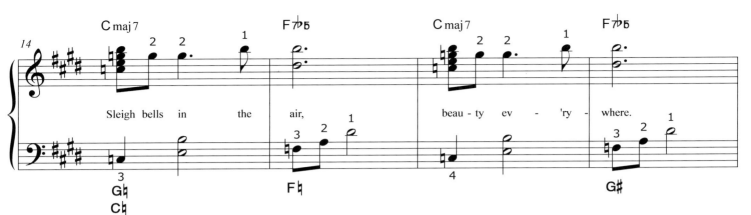

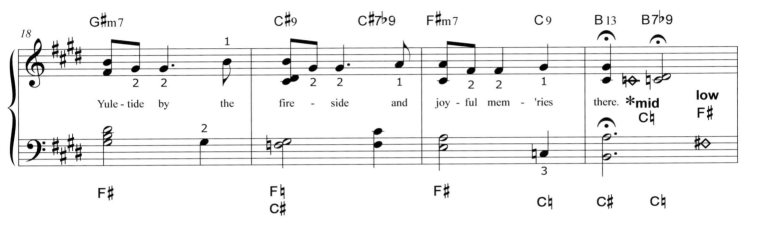

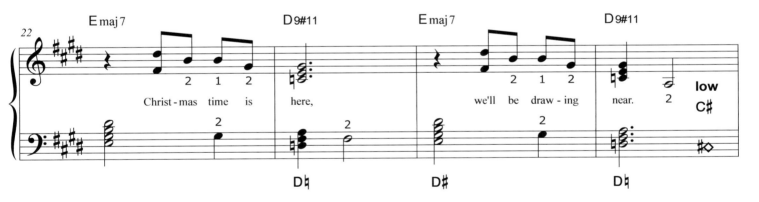

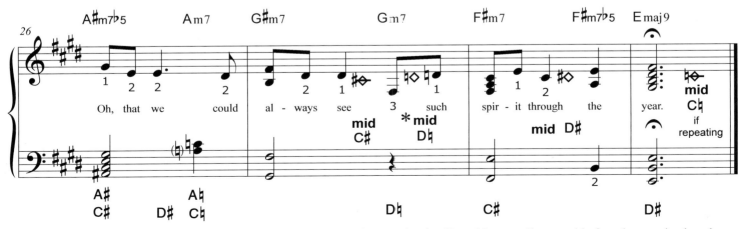

* The lever changes marked with an * in measures 10, 21 and 27 need to be flipped just a split second before the note is played.

3

Christmas Time Is Here

FROM A CHARLIE BROWN CHRISTMAS

for lever harps tuned to 3 flats

Music by VINCE GUARALDI
Words by LEE MENDELSON
Harp arrangement by SYLVIA WOODS

Set your sharping levers for the key signature, and then re-set the levers shown above.
Sharping lever changes are indicated with diamond notes and also with octave wording.
The lever changes marked with an * in measures 10, 21 and 27 need to be flipped just a split second before the note is played.

If you tune your lever harp to C or 1 or 2 flats, you should play the version on page 1 instead of this arrangement.

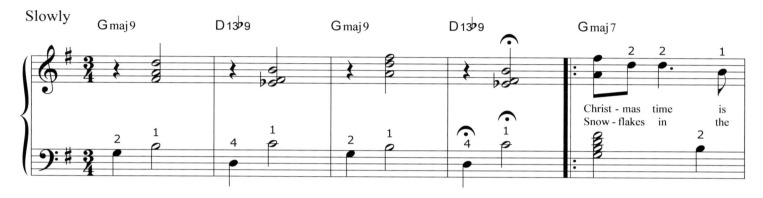

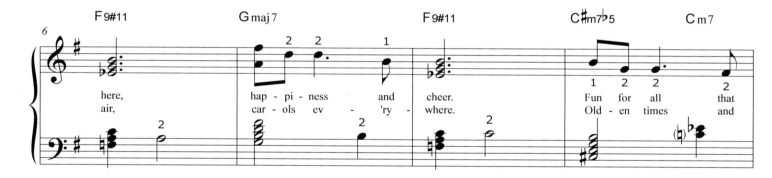

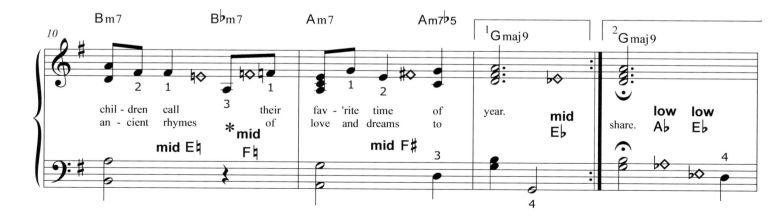

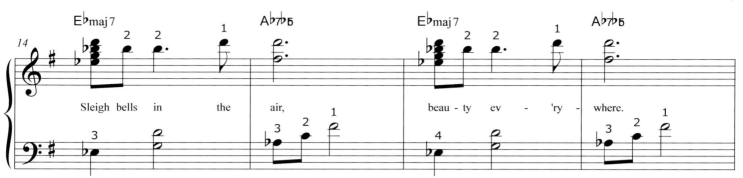

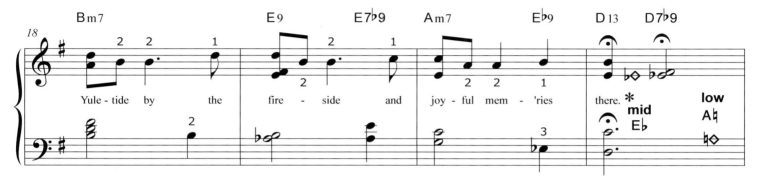

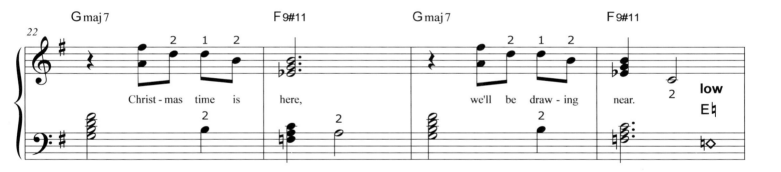

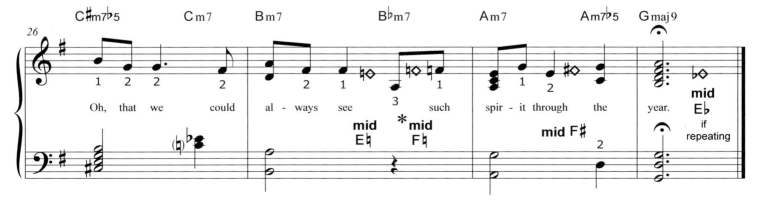

* The lever changes marked with an * in measures 10, 21 and 27 need to be flipped just a split second before the note is played.

LINUS AND LUCY

Intermediate lever or pedal harp arrangement

By VINCE GUARALDI
Harp arrangement by SYLVIA WOODS

Lever harp players: Set your levers as shown above. Cs and Fs not shown in the chart are not used in this arrangement.
There are no lever changes required within the piece.
Pedal harp players: set the C pedal as natural. Pedal changes are written below the bass staff.

Play the left hand lower on the strings than usual. All chords should be played flat, and not arpeggiated.

Moderately fast, with a feel of 2 beats per measure

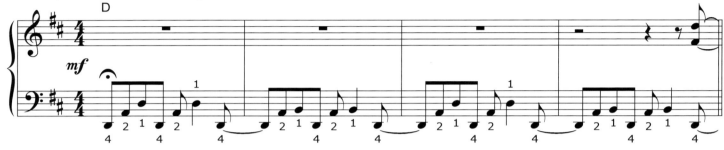

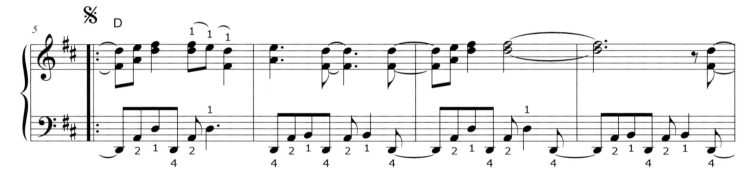

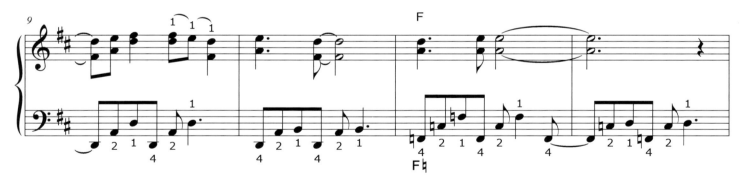

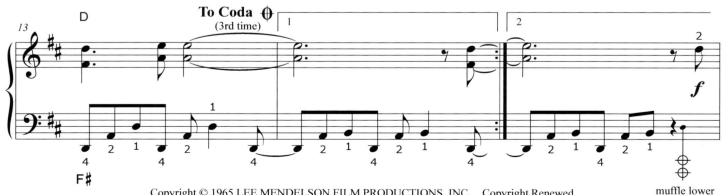

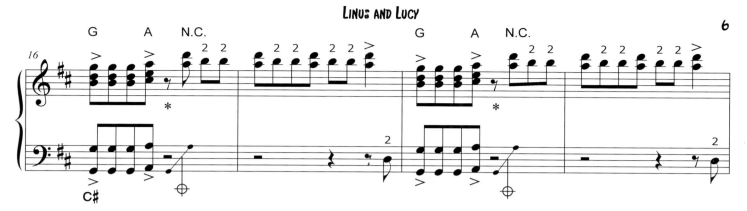

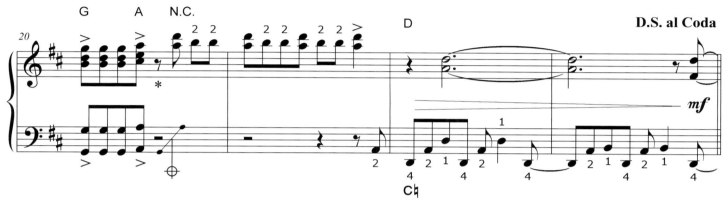

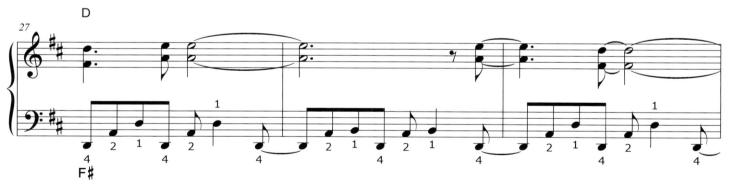

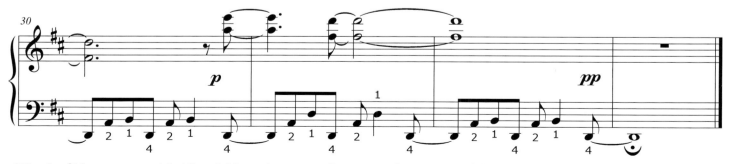

*On the 𝄾 in measures 16, 18 and 20, replace your fingers on the 3 notes of the A chord to muffle them.
In the left hand, muffle the bass notes as indicated.

Linus and Lucy

Advanced beginner arrangement, playable on small lever harps

By VINCE GUARALDI
Harp arrangement by SYLVIA WOODS

Lever harp players: Set your levers as shown above. Cs and Fs not shown in the chart are not used in this arrangement. There are no lever changes required within the piece.

Play the left hand lower on the strings than usual. All chords should be played flat, and not arpeggiated.

Moderately fast, with a feel of 2 beats per measure

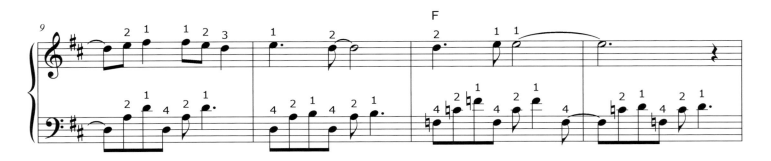

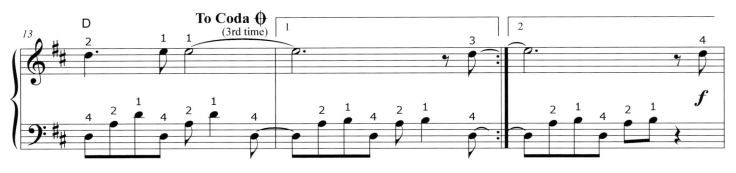

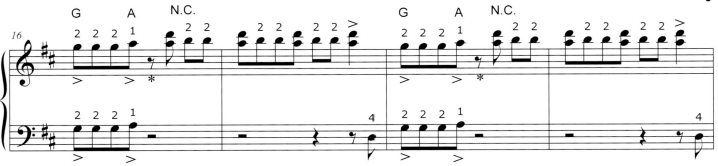

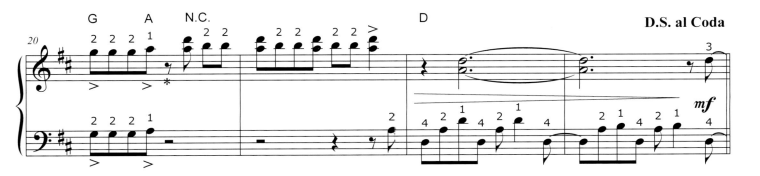

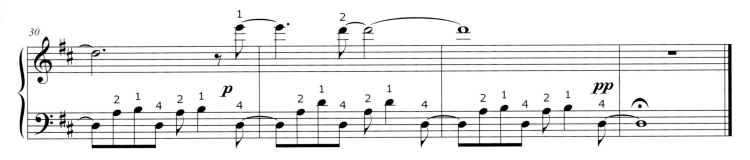

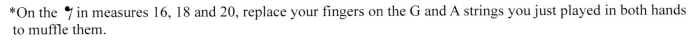

*On the ⅞ in measures 16, 18 and 20, replace your fingers on the G and A strings you just played in both hands to muffle them.

A Charlie Brown Christmas

A Charlie Brown Christmas was the first prime-time animated TV special based upon Charles Schulz's beloved *Peanuts* characters. Since its CBS debut in 1965, it has aired in the USA every Christmas season. *Christmas Time Is Here* was sung by members of the choir of St. Paul's Episcopal Church in San Rafael, California.

Linus and Lucy was originally released on the Vince Guaraldi Trio's album "Jazz Impressions of a Boy Named Charlie Brown" in 1964. It was used in the TV special A Charlie Brown Christmas, and has been featured in many subsequent specials. This happy dance tune is the most-recognized theme song of the *Peanuts* characters.

More Harp Arrangements of Pop Music by Sylvia Woods

All of Me
Beauty and the Beast
Music from Disney-Pixar's Brave
Bring Him Home from Les Misérables
Castle on a Cloud from Les Misérables
Dead Poets Society
John Denver Love Songs
76 Disney Songs
Fields of Gold
Fireflies
Music from Disney Frozen
Groovy Songs of the 60s
Four Holiday Favorites
House at Pooh Corner

Into the West from The Lord of the Rings
Lennon and McCartney
My Heart Will Go On from Titanic
Over the Rainbow from The Wizard of Oz
River Flows in You
22 Romantic Songs
Safe & Sound
Say Something
Stairway to Heaven
Music from Disney Tangled
A Thousand Years
Andrew Lloyd Webber Music
The Wizard of Oz
Theme from Disney-Pixar's Up

Available from harp music retailers and www.harpcenter.com

Sylvia Woods Harp Center
P.O. Box 223434, Princeville, HI 96722 U.S.A.

U.S. $11.99

8 88680 02730 8

HL00131539

ISBN 978-0-936661-68-1

9 780936 661681

EXCLUSIVELY DISTRIBUTED BY
HAL•LEONARD® CORPORATION
7777 W. BLUEMOUND RD. P.O. BOX 13819
MILWAUKEE, WISCONSIN 53213

With many thanks to Paul Baker and Heidi Spiegel